*Presented by:*

_____

*To:*

_____

*Date:*

_____

*Occasion:*

_____

# No Thorn
# Without a Rose

## "99 Words to Live By"

A series of fine gift books that presents inspirational words by renowned authors and captivating thinkers. Thought-provoking proverbs from many peoples and traditions complete each volume's collection.

"99 Words to Live By" explores topics that have moved and will continue to move people's hearts. Perfect for daily reflection as well as moments of relaxation.

# No Thorn
# Without a Rose

## 99 Sayings
## by Chiara Lubich

*edited by*

Julian Ciabattini

**New City Press**
**Hyde Park, New York**

Published in the United States by New City Press
202 Cardinal Rd., Hyde Park, NY 12538
©2008 New City Press (English translation)

Original Italian texts (see Sources on p. 110)
©Citta' Nuova Editrice, Rome, Italy

Cover design by Leandro De Leon

Library of Congress Cataloging-in-Publication Data:

A copy of the CIP data is available from the
Library of Congress.

ISBN 978-1-56548-294-4 (hardcover)
ISBN 978-1-56548-295-1 (paperback)

Printed in the United States of America

"The book of light that God is writing in my soul has two aspects: A luminous page of mysterious love: Unity. A luminous page of mysterious suffering: Jesus forsaken.

They are two faces of the same coin."

*(Chiara Lubich, 30 March 1948)*

In these few inspired words, Chiara expresses clearly the fundamental elements of her spirituality, a spirituality of unity, of communion, which has touched the lives of millions of people in 182 countries.

Speaking to participants at the 35th Conference of Bishops, Friends of the Focolare, John Paul II underlined the importance of rediscovering an "authentic spirituality of communion," the hallmark of the Movement:

We are faced with a demanding mission: to make the Church the place where the mystery of divine love is lived and the school where it is taught. How will this be possible without the rediscovery of an authentic spirituality of communion? We must first of all perceive with the eyes of our hearts the Trinitarian mystery present within us, so that we may then be able to discern it in the faces of others. Our brother or sister in faith is to be considered as "one who is a part of us" in the mysterious unity of the Mystical Body. Only by "making room" for my brothers and sisters, in order to see the positive in them, is it possible to grasp how much each of them is a gift for me ... Lived in this way, the spirituality of unity and communion which characterizes your Movement will not fail to bear prolific fruits of renewal for all believers.

*(John Paul II, 14 February 2001)*

I spent the first twenty-three years of my life in the beautiful and culturally rich region of Tuscany. Then, in the late 1960s, I went to Rome for a youth rally sponsored by the Focolare. Although I had known very little about the Movement, my encounter there with Chiara Lubich and her charism proved to be the turning point of my life.

I discovered that God is Love, that the gospel can be lived concretely in everyday life, and consequently that I too am called to be love.

Since that first encounter, the spirituality of unity, this new charism sent through Chiara to the Church and to all humankind, has enlightened and sustained my personal journey to God and opened my heart to the God within every person I meet.

I have spent most of my life with the Focolare community in North America, first in Toronto then in New York. Sharing the spirituality of unity with people of the most varied cultural backgrounds, of the most varied races and religions, has been a special gift from God for which I can never be grateful enough.

I hope that the selections chosen for this book may inspire many to follow God's universal call to love and " ... open ourselves to the reality of being one human family in one Father: God."

*Julian Ciabattini*

The words of the gospel are unique, fascinating, carefully scripted, and can be translated into life. They are light for everyone who comes into this world; they are universal.

There is no human
situation that does
not find an explicit
or implicit solution in that
small book that contains
the word of God.

Have you noticed that if you fail to learn the alphabet and the basic rules of grammar in primary school, you remain illiterate all your life, unable to read or write despite having intelligence and will?

In the same way if we do not learn to assimilate one by one the words of life that Jesus has pronounced in the gospel, even though we are "good Christians," we remain "gospel illiterates," unable to write with our lives: Christ.

Just as the entire Jesus
is in the sacred host and
in every single particle,
so the entire Jesus is
in the gospel and
in every one of his words.

When a girl knows she is loved, her life changes: everything around her seems more beautiful and every aspect of life is enhanced. She feels more kindly disposed toward others.

Infinitely more powerful is the experience of the Christian who comes to a more profound understanding of the truth that *God is love*.

Fall in love with God!
There are so many
beautiful things on earth!
God is even
more beautiful!

God-Love,
*believing in his love,*
*responding to his love*
*by loving,* these are
the great imperatives today.

*Love that which does not die!
Love the One who is Love!*
Love Him who in the evening of your life will look only at your tiny heart. You will be alone with him in that moment: dreadfully sad for the one whose heart is filled with vanity, immensely happy for the one whose heart is filled with the infinite love of God!

The stars shine
in the sky and the earth
stays in existence because
they are in motion:
movement is the life
of the universe.
People are truly happy
only if they turn on
the motor of their lives,
love, and keep it running.

The world needs
an invasion of love
and this depends
on each one of us.

One thing alone is
beautiful, lovable,
attractive, useful, radiant:
*what God wants*
*of you in the*
*present moment.*

Loving God on earth
means loving his will,
so that after a life in
his divine service
you will see him and
be with him forever.

You must never turn back, but forge always ahead.

Your life has been as it has been. God knows it.

The important thing is that the present, the only thing in your hands, not escape you. In it love God with all your heart, doing his will.

Look at the sun and its rays.

The sun is a symbol of the will of God, which is God himself. The rays are the will of God for each individual.

Walk toward the sun in the light of your ray, different and distinct from every other ray, and fulfill the particular, wonderful plan God wants from you.

There is an infinite number of rays, all coming from the same sun: a single will, particular for each person.

The closer the rays come to the sun, the closer they come to one another. We too, the closer we come to God, by doing the will of God more and more perfectly, the closer we come to one another.

Until we are all one.

The greatest wisdom
is to spend our time living
the will of God perfectly
in the present moment.

The purpose of a
Christian's life on earth
is to achieve sanctity.
Paul says this clearly
in speaking to the
Thessalonians:
"For this is the will of God,
your sanctification"
(1 Thes 4:3).

If you were a student and by chance came to know the questions of the school's final exams, you would consider yourself lucky and study the answers thoroughly.

Life is a trial and at the end it, too, has to pass an exam; but the infinite love of God has already told humanity what the questions will be: "For I was hungry and you gave me food, I was thirsty and you gave me drink" (Mt 25:35). The works of mercy will be the subject of the exam, those works in which God sees if you love him truly, having served him in your brothers and sisters.

My God, let me be
in this world the tangible
sacrament of your Love,
of your being Love;
let me be your arms
that press to themselves
and consume in love all the
loneliness of the world.

Like another Eucharist, let yourself "be eaten" by your neighbors. Put your entire self at their service, which is service to God, and your neighbors will come to you and love you. The fulfillment of God's every desire lies in fraternal love …

We need to enlarge our heart to the measure of the heart of Jesus. How much work that means! Yet this is the only thing necessary. When this is done, all is done. It means loving everyone we meet as God loves them. And since we live in time, we must love our neighbors one by one, without holding in our heart any left-over affection for the brother or sister met a moment before. It is the same Jesus, after all, whom we love in everyone.

In love what counts is to love. This is what it is like here on earth. Love (I speak of supernatural love which does not exclude natural love) is both so simple and so complex. It demands that you do your part and awaits the other's.

If you try to live only for love, you will realize that here on earth it is worthwhile doing your part. You do not know whether the other part will ever come; and it is not necessary that it should ... you will never be discouraged if you convince yourself that in love what counts is to love.

And you love Jesus in your neighbor, Jesus who always returns to you, maybe in other ways.

There are those who do things "for love." There are those who do things trying "to be Love." Those who do things "for love" may do them well, but, thinking they are doing great service for their neighbor, who is sick for instance, they may annoy with their chatter, their advice and with their help. Such charity is burdensome and inappropriate.

They may gain merit, but the other is left with a burden. This is why it is necessary to "be Love."

Our destiny is like
that of the planets:
if they revolve, they are;
if they do not, they are not.
We are, in the sense that
the life of God, not our life,
lives in us, if we do not stop
loving for one moment.

Mercy is the ultimate
expression of charity,
and is that which fulfills it.

The presence of charity in the world is like the sun's appearance in spring. The barren earth may seem to have nothing to offer, but suddenly all is green again, and flowers are blooming. Their seeds were always there, but the warmth was lacking.

Goodwill and good intentions exist in the world, but we often do not see their fruits. Without the flame of charity, they could not come to the light.

Friendship or kindness toward others is not enough for Jesus, neither philanthropy nor solidarity alone. The kind of love that Jesus asks for is more than nonviolence.

It is something active, dynamic. He asks that we no longer live for ourselves but for others.

Love for neighbor also means putting ourselves inside them as best we can, so as to share their sorrow and joy, making ourselves "one with them" like Saint Paul: "To the weak I became weak ... I have become all things to all."

Make *yourself one.* These important words express *the* way of loving. What do these three little words mean and what do they require of us? When we are filled with apprehension, with judgments or with thoughts ... of anything else, we are unable to enter into the heart of others to understand them, to accept them and share their sorrows. "Making yourself one" requires of us poverty of spirit. Only then is unity possible.

Nothing is small
if it is done out of love.

Do you know
what you should do when
you have loved and
loved and loved?
Love some more!

The first Christians are not
remembered so much for
going into ecstasy
but for how much they
loved one another:
they had grasped,
in its first freshness,
the testament of Jesus.

Just as two poles of electricity, even when there is a current, do not produce light until they are joined together, likewise two persons cannot experience the light of this charism until they are united in Christ through charity.

Christ is love and a Christian must be love. Love generates communion: communion as the basis of the Christian life and as its summit.

In this communion a person no longer goes to God alone but travels in company. This a fact of incomparable bea that makes our soul repea e words of the Scripture ow very good and pleas t is when kindred live t er in unity!" (Ps 133:l).

The person next to me was created as a gift for me and I was created as a gift for the person next to me. On earth all stands in a relationship of love with all: each thing with each thing. We have to be Love, however, to discover the golden thread among all things that exist.

Jesus is the Word of God made man in order to teach us to live according to the model of trinitarian life, the same life he lives in the bosom of the Father.

He was not content with simply underlining and linking to one another the two fundamental commandments of the Old Testament: "You shall love the Lord, your God, with all your heart, with all your soul, and with all your mind.... You shall love your neighbor as yourself" (Mt 22:37-39). Instead, he teaches us the commandment, which he himself does not hesitate to call "his" and "new," and by means of which we can live the life of the Trinity here on earth: "Love one another as I have loved you" (see Jn 13:34; 15:12).

The book of light that God is writing in my soul has two aspects: a luminous page of mysterious love: Unity. A luminous page of mysterious suffering: Jesus forsaken. They are two faces of the same coin.

Before all else, the soul must always fix its gaze on the one Father of many children. Then it must see all as children of the same Father. In mind and in heart we must always go beyond the bounds imposed on us by human life alone and create the habit of constantly opening ourselves to the reality of being one human family in one Father: God.

The world today is beset with tensions: between North and South, in the Middle East, in Africa. There are wars, threats of new conflicts and many other evils characteristic of our age. Yet, in spite of all that, paradoxically the world is moving today toward unity and consequently toward peace; it is a sign of the times.

Jesus, our model,
taught us two things alone,
and which are one:
to be children of only one
Father and to be
brothers and sisters
to each other.

When Christ is there
in the unity of
brothers and sisters,
the world believes.

When unity among us
becomes difficult,
we must not break,
but bend, until
love makes the miracle
of one heart and one soul.

Better what is less perfect,
but in unity with our
brothers and sisters,
than what is more perfect,
but in disunity with them,
because perfection
does not lie in ideas
or in wisdom,
but in charity.

Every soul that wants to achieve unity must claim only one right: To serve everyone, because in everyone the soul serves God.... It must live constantly "emptied" because it is totally "in love" with God's will ... and in love with the will of its neighbor, who it wants to serve for God. A servant does only what his or her Master commands.

If we are united, Jesus is among us. And this has value. It is worth more than any other treasure that our heart may possess; more than mother, father, brothers, sisters, children. It is worth more than our house, our work...more than our business deals; more than nature which surrounds us with flowers and fields, the sea and the stars; more than our own soul.

It is he who, inspiring his saints with his eternal truths, leaves his mark upon every age.

This too is his hour. Not so much the hour of a saint but of him, of *him among us*, of him living in us as we build up — in the unity of love — his Mystical Body ... Make one of all and in all the One.

Unity!
Who would dare
speak of it?
It is ineffable as God.
You feel it, see it,
rejoice over it but ...
it is ineffable!
All enjoy its presence,
all suffer its absence.
It is peace, joy, love, ardor,
and the spirit of heroism,
of boundless generosity.
It is Jesus among us.

The purpose of the Eucharist: to make us God (by participation). By mixing our flesh with Christ's life-giving flesh, which is given life by the Holy Spirit, the Eucharist divinizes us in soul and body. Therefore it makes us God.

Now God can only stay in God. This is why the Eucharist makes the human being, who is fed with it worthily, enter the bosom of the Father; it places the human being in the Trinity in Jesus.

At the same time the Eucharist does not do this only for the individual person, but for many persons who, all being God, are not many, but one. They are God and they are all together in God…. Now this reality, which the Eucharist brings about, is the Church.

The diameter of a tree's foliage often corresponds to the diameter of its roots. A soul expands in Christ's charity to the extent of the suffering it has offered for him.

Nothing good, useful
or fruitful is accomplished
in the world without
knowing how
to accept fatigue
and suffering, in a word,
the cross.

It was the Holy Spirit, we believe, before leading us into the mystery of unity, who concentrated our faith and all of our love in Jesus who … in an insuperable climax of love and suffering, cries out from the cross: "My God, my God, why have you forsaken me?" (Mk 15:34; Mt 27:46).

In that moment he experienced the most profound separation that can ever be imagined; in a sense, he experienced being separated from his Father with whom he was and remained one. At the same time, he gives all humankind a new and fuller unity than the one lost through sin: he reunites all with one another and with God in a new unity, which is a participation in his unity with the Father and with us.

So that we might have Light,
you ceased to see.
So that we might have union,
you experienced separation
from the Father.
So that we might possess
wisdom, you made
yourself "ignorance."
So that we might be clothed
with innocence,
you made yourself "sin."
So that God might be in us,
you felt him far from you.

I have only one
Spouse on earth:
Jesus forsaken.
I have no other
God but him.
In him there is the
whole of paradise with the
Trinity and the whole of the
earth with humanity.

I am convinced that unity in its deepest, most intimate and spiritual aspect, can be understood only by those who have chosen as their portion in life ... Jesus forsaken who cries out, "My God, my God, why have you forsaken me?"

Forget everything ...
even the most
sublime things;
let yourself be ruled
by one single Idea,
by the one God alone
who must penetrate
every fiber of your being:
by Jesus crucified.

Believe it, one minute
of your life on that sickbed,
if you accept it as
a gift of God,
is worth more than all the
words of a preacher
who may speak a lot,
but loves God little.

Those who know Love and unite their suffering to the sufferings of Jesus on the cross, letting their own drop of blood lose itself in the sea of Christ's divine blood, have the most honored place human beings can hold: to be like God come down on earth: redeemer of the world ...

There is nothing, perhaps, more puzzling, more difficult to grasp than the cross; it does not penetrate the head and the heart of human beings. It does not penetrate because it is not understood, because often we have become Christians only in name, merely baptized, maybe practicing, yet immensely far from being what Jesus would like us to be.

The cross. It is such a common thing. It is so faithful that it never misses its appointment every day. To take up this cross is all we need to make us saints.

The soul understands that the life of Jesus does not culminate in the way of the cross and in death, but in the resurrection and the ascension to heaven.

Then the human way of seeing things fades and becomes meaningless, and bitterness no longer poisons the brief joys of this earthly life. For the soul that proverb so full of melancholy, "There is no rose without a thorn," means nothing. But because of the wave of the revolution of love into which God has drawn the soul, the exact opposite is true: "There is no thorn without a rose."

Jesus Forsaken, embraced, locked to one's self, wanted as our only all, he consumed in *one with us, we consumed in one* with him, made suffering with him Suffering: here lies everything. Here is how we become (by participation) God, Love.

Only those who pass
through the ice of suffering
reach the fire of love.

One day, urged I think by the Holy Spirit, I went into church, and with my heart full of trust, I asked: "Why did you wish to remain on earth, on every point of the earth, in the most sweet Eucharist, and you have not found, you who are God, also a way to bring and to leave here Mary, the mother of all of us who journey?"

And from the tabernacle, in the silence he seemed to reply: "I have not left her because I want to see her again in you. Even if you are not immaculate, my love will virginize you, and you, all of you, will open your arms and hearts as mothers of humanity, which, as in times past, thirsts for God and for his mother.

If when
praying the rosary
sometimes a living stream
of heaven seems to flow
around us, and the world,
as beautiful as it is, pales
before such enchantment,
what will it be like
to meet you, Mary?

A mother is more the object of the heart's intuition than of the mind's speculation. She is more poetry than philosophy, because she is too real and profound, close to the human heart.

So it is with Mary, the Mother of mothers, who the sum of all the affection, goodness, and mercy of all the mothers in the world cannot manage to equal.

Mary is peaceful like nature, pure, serene, clear, temperate, beautiful.... She brings the divine to earth as gently as a heavenly plane sloping from the dizzy heights of heaven to the infinite smallness of creatures. She is the Mother of all and of each human being, who alone knows how to burble and smile at her child in such a way that, even though it is small, each knows how to enjoy her caress and respond with its love to *that love*.

What characterized Mary, though in her unique perfection, should characterize every Christian: to repeat Christ, the Truth, with the personality given to each by God.

Having fully carried out God's design for her, Mary now lives in heaven. She is the flower and the first fruit of the Church and of creation, which in her is already Christified and divinized. In a certain way, we can think of her as being set into the Trinity, through grace, the icon and expression of all creation.

Do you know what time
of day is most beautiful?
It is our prayer time,
when we are speaking
with the one we
love the most.

If Jesus died for me,
he is always thinking of me,
always loving me.
And I? I should always be
thinking of him,
always loving him.

Grant that I love you, Lord,
with an immense love
as immense as your love.
Grant that I love you, Lord,
with your own heart.

All my life
should be a love affair
with my Spouse.
All else is vanity.
All that is not
the word lived
is vanity.

We have an inner life and an outer life. One is the flowering of the other. One is the root of the other. One for the other brings forth the foliage of the tree of our life.

Our inner life is fed by our outer life. The more I enter into the soul of my brother or sister, the more I enter into God within me. The more I enter into God within me, the more I enter into my brother or sister.

God — myself — my brother or sister: it is all one world, all one kingdom....

O Holy Spirit, how much we ought to be grateful to you yet how little we are! That you are totally one with Jesus and the Father, to whom we more often turn, consoles us, but it is no excuse.

We want to be with you who are "of comforters the best; ... the soul's most welcome guest; sweet refreshment here below."

You are light, joy, beauty.

You seize and captivate souls, you inflame hearts, you inspire deep and decisive thoughts of sanctity with unexpected personal commitments.

You work what many sermons cannot teach.

You sanctify.

If a soul gives itself to God sincerely, he works on it. And love and suffering are the raw materials of his divine game — suffering to dig abysses in the soul, love to soothe the suffering and still more love that fills the soul, giving it the equilibrium of peace.

Who is in the Father, having come to him from a long history of sin, out of God's pure mercy is equal in his eyes to the innocent who has arrived there by dint of love.

In fact, the moment you recognize yourself as a sinner, and delight (by loving God more than your own soul, and this is pure love) in being similar to him made sin, you fill the emptiness left by sin.

In this way you arrive in heaven through God's pure mercy (which means having received everything for free) but at the same time out of pure love for God spoken freely by your heart.

Let me be grateful —
at least a little —
in the time that is left
to me for the love
you have poured upon me
and that has compelled
me to tell you:
I love you.

We must play the part
of Jesus here on earth.
We need to lend God
our humanity so that he
may use it to have his
beloved Son
live once again.

Charity is preserved
by truth, and truth is pure
mercy with which we
ought to be clothed
from head to foot
in order to be able to call
ourselves Christians.

Nothing is more organized
than what love orders
and nothing is more free
than what love unites.

In these times, only an individual sanctity is not enough, nor one that is communitarian but closed. We must feel within ourselves the sorrow and also joy that Christ experiences today in his Bride.

We need to become saints as Church.

Virginity is so beautiful and sublime because, through it, human beings give to God the best thing they have: the possibility of extending their earthly lives through children (a need for humans, who *feel* the need *live on*). The virgin detaches self from the earth like a flower that does not wish to develop into fruit here below but continues to carry the seed. Instead, a virgin ascends to heaven in order to be planted and bloom permanently there.

The virgin gives witness to *God* just by the gift of virginity, because there is no earthly reason to remain a virgin; it makes sense only in the light of heaven.

In the splendid garden of the Church all the virtues have flowered and still flower. The founders of the religious orders each exemplify a particular virtue; they are all making their way to heaven, transfigured by great love and suffering like a "word of God."

$B$egin again always.
Improve always.

Time is fast escaping me; accept, O Lord, my life! In my heart I hold you, the treasure that must shape every move I make. Follow me, watch over me; yours is my loving: rejoicing and suffering. May no one catch even a sigh. Hidden in your tabernacle I live, I work for all. May the touch of my hand be yours, only yours be the tone of my voice. In this rag of myself may your Love return to this arid world, with the water that gushes abundantly from your wound, O Lord!

There is a word of the gospel that ... sums up all that we should do in life. It recapitulates all the laws that God has inscribed in the depths of every human heart.

Listen to it: "Do to others as you would have them do to you; for this is the law and the prophets."

This is the "Golden Rule."

"**D**o to others as you would have them do to you."

Let us love every neighbor we meet during the day like this.

Let us imagine we are in others' situations, treating them as we would want to be treated in their place.

The voice of God within us will suggest how to express the love appropriate to every situation.

## Reflections of Light
## upon the World

At times it is thought that the gospel does not resolve all human problems and that, instead, it simply brings about the kingdom of God understood in a strictly religious sense. But it is not so. Certainly, it is not the historical Jesus who resolves today's problems. It is Jesus-us, members of his Mystical Body, Jesus-me, Jesus-you…. It is Jesus present in each person, in that given person — when his grace and love live in him or her — who constructs a bridge or builds a road. It is Jesus, the true and most profound personality of every person. And it is as another Christ that the Christian brings his or her characteristic contribution to all fields, whether in science, in art, in politics.

Unity lived among us must be brought into our political parties, among the parties, into the various political institutions and into every sphere of public life and into the relationships among nations.

Then the people of all nations will be able to rise above their borders and look beyond, loving the others' country as their own.

Politics is the love of all loves, gathering the resources of people and groups into the unity of a common design so as to provide the means for each one to fulfill in complete freedom his or her specific vocation. But it also encourages people to co-operate, bringing together needs and resources, questions and answers, instilling mutual trust among all. Politics can be compared to the stem of a flower, which supports and nourishes the fresh unfolding of the petals of the community.

We are filled with wonder that the Word of God having become man, during the years of his private life did not only retreat into solitude to meditate and pray, but he chose to be a worker. This choice makes us see how important work is in the mind of God and how much it constitutes the make-up of a human being. Without it a human being would be considered less human.

Thus, human beings are fulfilled precisely through their work.

Give, give; put "giving" into practice. Create and increase the culture of giving.

Give our surplus or even what we ourselves need, if our heart urges us to do so. Give to those who do not have, knowing that this way of using what we have reaps an infinite return, because our giving opens God's hands, and he, in his providence, fills us superabundantly so that we can give anew and receive anew and thus be able to meet the boundless needs of many.

The artist is perhaps
closest to the saint.
For if the saint is the miracle
of one who knows
how to give God to the world,
the artist gives,
in a certain way,
the most beautiful creature
of the earth:
the human soul.

Today we often hear the famous line of Dostoyevsky: "Beauty will save the world." ... But what is true beauty? It is God. God is not only good, that is, the Good, and true, the Truth, he is also Beauty. And beauty presented on its own, without containing in itself the good and the true, would not be true beauty.

We must offer the world true beauty.

The love that Jesus has in mind demands that we love everyone, making no distinction between the pleasant and the unpleasant, the attractive and the unattractive, the fellow countryman and the stranger, the person belonging to my church or to another, to my religion or another. The love that Jesus has in mind encompasses everyone.

For those who wish
to commit themselves to
reconciliation, it is a duty
and therefore a key point for
any possible ecumenical
spirituality, to live the words
of the gospel, one by one,
to re-evangelize
our way of thinking,
of seeing, of loving.

An ecumenical spirituality will flourish to the degree that those dedicated to it see in the crucified and abandoned Jesus, who re-abandons himself to Father, the key to understanding every disunity and to recomposing unity.

When we, of the most various religions, enter into dialogue among ourselves, that is, when we are open to one another in a dialogue of human kindness, of mutual esteem, of respect, of mercy, we are also opening ourselves to God and, in the words of John Paul II, "we let God be present in our midst." … And what greater guarantee can there be than the presence of God, what greater help can there be for those who want to be instruments of fraternity and peace?

It is not true that today's youth have withdrawn into their own private world and, in general, have little interest in the large-scale problems of humankind.

There are many young people who, precisely because they are freer from conditioning and self-ish interests, because of their need to believe in something authentic, because they long to renew the world, are sensitive to great ideals. And often among the young there is the most compelling and fascinating response to the thrusts of history.

## The Art of Loving

Love, therefore, is one of the great secrets of this moment.

Love with a special love. Not, of course, with that love reserved only for your own family or friends, but with love for everyone, likeable or not, poor or rich, young or old, from your country or from another, friends or enemies … toward everyone.

And be the first to love, taking the initiative, without waiting to be loved.

And love not just with words, but practically, with actions.

And love one another.

Dearest young people, if you do this, if we all do this, universal brotherhood will widen, solidarity will flourish, goods will be better distributed, and over the world will shine the rainbow of peace, a world which, in a few years, will be in your hands.

## The Great Attraction
## of Modern Times

This is the great attraction of modern times: to penetrate to the highest contemplation while mingling with everyone, one person alongside others. I would say even more: to lose oneself in the crowd in order to fill it with the divine, like a piece of bread dipped in wine. I would say even more: made sharers in God's plans for humanity, to embroider patterns of light on the crowd, and at the same time to share with our neighbor shame, hunger, troubles, brief joys. Because the attraction of our times, as of all times, is the highest conceivable expression of the human and the divine, Jesus and Mary: the Word of God, a carpenter's son; the Seat of Wisdom, mother at home.

## Sources

(The numbers refer to the selection number in the present book, followed by the page number in the cited work by Chiara Lubich.)

*Essential Writings:*
*Spirituality • Dialogue • Culture*
(Hyde Park, NY: New City Press, 2007)

1:7; 2:7; 3:127; 4:127; 5:55; 6:57; 7:56; 8:59; 9:171; 10:171; 11:76; 12:58; 13:75; 14:76; 15:70; 16:71; 17:79; 18:82; 19:81; 20:81; 21:82; 22:84; 23:84; 24:85; 25:86; 26:365; 29:87; 30:87; 31:87; 32:31; 33:100; 34:87; 35:205; 36:25; 37:17-18; 38:12; 39:18; 40:7; 41:108; 42:109; 43:18; 44:102; 45:108; 46:129; 47:96; 48:14; 49:206; 50:94; 51:95; 52:25; 53:21; 54:23; 55:23; 56:89-90; 57:91; 58:89; 59:96; 60:96; 61:43; 62:47; 63:135; 64:135; 65:40; 66:207; 67:64; 68:61; 69:62; 70:127; 71:64-65; 72:144; 73:153; 74:97; 75:133; 76:177; 77:101; 78:109; 79:118; 80:118; 81:114; 82:75; 83:75; 84:121; 85:122; 86:240; 87:243; 88:254-255; 89:286; 90:281; 91:305; 92:318; 94:328; 95:329; 96:343; 97:362; 98:368; 99:169

*The Art of Loving*
(Hyde Park, NY: New City Press, scheduled to be published in 2009.)

27, 28, 93

## Wings for the Soul
*99 Sayings on Happiness*
hardcover: 978-1-56548-283-8
softcover: 978-1-56548-284-5

## We Have Seen a Great Light
*99 Sayings on Christmas*
hardcover: 978-1-56548-270-8
paperback: 978-56548-271-5

## The Golden Thread of Life
*99 Sayings on Love*
hardcover: 978-1-56548-182-4

## Blessed Are the Peacemakers
*99 Sayings on Peace*
hardcover: 978-1-56548-183-1

## Sunshine On Our Way
*99 Sayings on Friendship*
hardcover: 978-1-56548-195-4

Organizations and Corporations

This title is available at special quantity discounts for bulk purchases for sales promotions, premiums, or fundraising.
For information call or write:

New City Press, Marketing Dept.
202 Cardinal Rd.
Hyde Park, NY 12538.
Tel: 1-800-462-5980;
1-845-229-0335
Fax: 1-845-229-0351
info@newcitypress.com